THE 4 C'S FORMULA

Thanks to the Creative Team:

Kerri Morrison

Hamish MacDonald

Shannon Waller

Jennifer Bhatthal

Christine Nishino

Willard Bond

Paul Hamilton

The 4 C's Formula

Have you ever wondered why some people are super-achievers and seem to go from success to success while others never seem to get out of the starting blocks?

In my 40 years of coaching high-achieving entrepreneurs, I've noticed that they all go through a process to help them break through to the next level of success. I call this process The 4 C's Formula.

The 4 C's Formula is a universal process that can be used by anyone who wants to achieve greater success in any part of their life.

Mindset is key!
Score yourself on your 4 C's Formula mindset as well as seven other ambition mindsets using the fold-out scorecard at the back of this book.

Strategic Coach®, Strategic Coach® Program, Unique Ability®, The 4 C's Formula™, 10x Mind Expander®, and Self-Multiplying Company™ are trademarks of The Strategic Coach Inc.

Illustrations by Hamish MacDonald.

Printed in Toronto, Canada. The Strategic Coach Inc., 33 Fraser Avenue, Suite 201, Toronto, Ontario, M6K 3J9.

This publication is meant to strengthen your common sense, not to substitute for it. It is also not a substitute for the advice of your doctor, lawyer, accountant, or any of your advisors, personal or professional.

If you would like further information about the Strategic Coach® Program or other Strategic Coach® services and products, please telephone 416.531.7399 or 1.800.387.3206.

Library and Archives Canada Cataloguing in Publication

Sullivan, Dan, 1944-, author
        The 4 C's formula / Dan Sullivan.

ISBN 978-1-897239-40-7 (paperback)

        1. Goal (Psychology). 2. Success--Psychological aspects.
I. Title. II. Title: Four C's formula.

BF505.G6S93 2015   158.1   C2015-903648-8

Contents

Introduction

I was drafted into the army for the Vietnam War in 1965 when I was 21 years old. Back in the draft days, as long as you were a full-time student, they couldn't draft you, but I had dropped out of college for a year and I lost my deferment.

During basic training, we learned battlefield skills, and part of this process was practice with live hand grenades.

The sergeant who was in charge took us through the procedure the night before. Essentially, each of us would have to take a turn going down into a pit with a big mound of dirt in front of us. We would take the pin out of the grenade, which would mean it was then live. There's a lever that keeps it from going off, but the moment you release it, there's a five- or six-second fuse and then the grenade explodes. By that time, we were supposed to have thrown it over the mound where it would explode on the other side so none of the fragments would hit us or anyone else.

Horror stories to focus our minds.

The sergeant told us some horror stories of people dropping the grenade during the exercise. Mistakes happen in basic training, and people do get killed. They tell you the stories because they want to impress upon you that you can't fool around with the weapons.

We were told that in the pit with us would be a trained person who, if anything went wrong, would know what to do. It's a very serious job, as you can imagine, because for one reason or another, some people would get nervous and they would drop the grenade.

That night was a bad night for all of us, and I didn't get much sleep. You anticipate what would happen if you really

screwed up. You are dead, literally, if you cannot do it.

The next morning, we appeared before the sergeant and he asked, "Is anyone scared?"

In a group of 50 men, I was the only one who raised my hand.

Telling the truth about scary situations.

The sergeant said, "Sullivan is the only person here I trust because he's actually telling me what's going on. He's actually telling the truth."

He went on, "There's no dishonor in saying that you're scared. As a matter of fact, people who are scared and don't say they're scared are a bigger worry to me than people who admit they're scared."

"As a result," he continued, "Sullivan is going to go first."

I went down into the pit and I performed according to instructions, and after the training exercise, the sergeant said:

"I want to tell you the difference between fear and courage: Fear is wetting your pants. Courage is doing what you're supposed to do with wet pants."

I never forgot that. Since then, I kept in mind that everybody experiences fear, but it's how you respond to the fear that makes the difference. There are only two options: There's courage and there's courage-avoidance. You're either courageous or you're indulging yourself in some sort of method or activity to avoid courage, which shows up as paralysis, procrastination, or, in some cases, addiction.

Courage-avoidance means you're not allowing yourself to actually experience something you're supposed to experience in order to grow to the next level. But having courage and pursuing a goal despite fear or discomfort is what moves you forward.

The absolutely crucial step in your growth formula.

In my decades of coaching successful entrepreneurs, and in my own entrepreneurial experience, I have found that courage is a key part of a formula that everyone must go through in order to achieve greater levels of capability and confidence.

If you look at anyone's life and identify where they're successful and where they're frustrated and failing, you'll immediately see that the crucial difference is the presence of courage or its absence. Intelligence is important, skill is important, and so is successful experience. But without courage, none of these will lead to transformative personal breakthroughs that can generate new kinds of growth in every area of your life.

Simple model that works every time.

That is what this book is about. I'm going to share with you the process that entrepreneurs follow to be constantly progressing toward bigger goals and breakthroughs in their lives. It's a very simple model, and you'll find it works every time. If you want to grow and take your business and life to the next level, this formula is yours to use.

Formula
How Every Breakthrough Happens

The 4 C's Formula is illustrated by a four-stage clockwise progression with Commitment as stage one, Courage as stage two, Capability as stage three, and Confidence as stage four.

Nothing starts until you commit to achieving a specific measurable result by a specific date in your future. After you've made the commitment, courage is required because you have to take action before you've acquired the capability to achieve the result. Capability is actually created because of your commitment and courage. And, finally, confidence is the result of these first three stages.

I first discovered this formula by observing one of my project managers, Cathy Davis, go through the process. Cathy is in all my workshops in the Strategic Coach Program, so she's very well known for what she does. The clients talk to her all the time about project management and how she sets up my teamwork. In fact, she's so extraordinarily good at what she does that when she moved 1,000 miles away, there was no question that I would continue working with her, and she has been able to coordinate all of her teamwork with me and the company remotely.

How commitment opens up possibilities.
A client of ours was putting together a virtual conference that included video presentations that were produced beforehand. This client approached Cathy and asked her to do a video presentation on project management and how she gets teams together to work for me. She immediately committed to do it, but soon started getting the jitters as

she'd never created a video before.

She came to me and said, "I don't know if I can do this."

I said, "Well, you committed to it." She agreed. And I said, "You're just realizing that you committed to something you don't yet have the capability and confidence to do."

I asked if she really wanted to call the client and tell him that she didn't want to do it. She said, "No, no, no. I'll do it, but I'm scared."

Cathy went into the studio, and she had a tough time. It took about twice as long as was scheduled to record the presentation. It was beautifully edited in the end, but it was a very difficult afternoon for her.

She came out of the studio and said, "Boy, I don't know if I want to do that again."

Courage immediately grows a bigger future.

Yet the next morning, she came in and said, "I'm going to do another presentation." She went into the studio to record a new video and nailed it in one take. This time, when she came out of the booth, she was flying sky-high. Over a 48-hour period, she had gone from fear to confidence.

After thinking about what she experienced, I sent Cathy an email that said, "Commitment leads to Courage. Courage leads to Capability. Capability leads to Confidence. Confidence leads to Commitment. Apply, lather, rinse, repeat."

She wrote back and said, "That's perfect." She told me that she felt a tremendous amount of gratitude from my encouragement and from having the process laid out like that in front of her. She felt that next time she could move through the same process and feel more comfortable doing it. It dispelled the mystery of what she had gone through. She knew there would be times when she needed to go through the process again, but because she now had a name for it and for all the stages she went through, it didn't seem as daunting.

Instant process for entrepreneurial growth.

I realized on the spot that I'd created a new process for entrepreneurs to describe what they were experiencing. The next day, I put it together in a four-box form, and we introduced it into the following quarter's workshops.

The 4 C's Formula was a big hit right off the bat. What I got the entrepreneurs to do, first of all, was to take some area in their past where they had achieved a breakthrough and analyze their experience using the four boxes. I then had them get into small groups and tell each other their 4 C's stories.

When they were finished sharing, I said, "Okay. That's the past. Now let's pick something you're doing right now where you're currently in the courage stage." They went through the same process and documented it, this time looking toward the future.

I explained to them that everything about being an entrepreneur was in these four boxes.

Entrepreneurs teaching courage to others.

Most people won't take action on a project or goal until they feel capable and confident about it, but those are stages three and four of the process. You can't have confidence until you have created a new capability, and you can't acquire a new capability until you have first made a commitment and then gone through a period of courage. This four-stage process is the formula for all entrepreneurial breakthroughs.

And yet it need not be used solely by entrepreneurs. Indeed, The 4 C's Formula has proven to be a ground-breaking concept among those who've used it and shared it because of its universality. In addition to having real-life practicality in an entrepreneur's business, we're also seeing our clients in the Strategic Coach Program take this model home and teach it to their children. We have The 4 C's model outlined on cards that we give to our clients, and we tell them, "Go

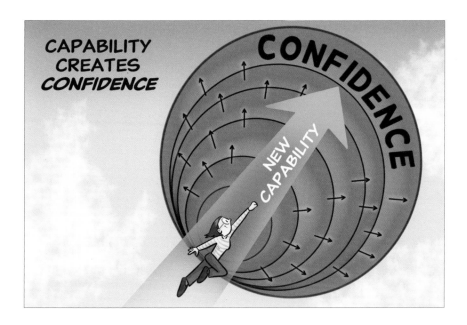

home and talk to your children about how they can practice The 4 C's in their lives."

Walking children through the formula.

One of our team members here at Coach, Tennyson, did that very thing. Tennyson has a 12-year-old daughter, and, for a variety of reasons, her daughter was having a difficult time adjusting to a new culture at a new school. To make matters worse, she came in partway through a term. What was being required of her in this new school was much greater and more challenging than anything she'd faced before.

Tennyson took the 4 C's card home and walked her daughter through the formula. She talked to her about what commitment was and had her daughter reiterate that she was really committed to doing this—she wasn't being forced to do it; she was committed. Tennyson explained to her that as a result of this commitment, she's now going through a period of courage where there are difficult adjustments to be made, but already capability is developing and it's going to lead to a new level of confidence.

The next day, there was a tremendous change in the girl's approach to what she was doing. Tennyson shared that her daughter's confidence had doubled or tripled since their talk the day before.

The 4 C's are the essence of entrepreneurism.
What was most significant for Tennyson's daughter was that The 4 C's Formula made the tough period she was going through an official part of a bigger process. In other words, she was allowed to name the experience, not as being some-thing wrong with her, but as what you have to do if you're going to jump to a higher level of capability and confidence.

It's necessary to go through a period of courage after making a commitment—and there's nothing wrong with feeling that fear.

Most of the entrepreneurs in the Strategic Coach Program are self-made people. They didn't inherit their companies— they created their companies. The vast majority of them didn't come from money, but now they have a lot of money. As a result, they're worried that their children won't develop entrepreneurial attitudes of their own.

The 4 C's Formula is an entryway for children to get intro-duced to the world of entrepreneurism. In essence, The 4 C's Formula is what entrepreneurism is all about.

Anytime someone is using The 4 C's Formula, whether they're an entrepreneur or not, they're being entrepreneurial. The process highlights what it is that makes an entrepreneur an entrepreneur. When they try to avoid this or try to make progress without taking these steps, they aren't actually entrepreneurs. They're faking it.

This formula is universal. It will start with entrepreneurs, but it can go everywhere. The moment people find that it's okay to go through a period of courage, they produce really big things. The formula tells them, "Of course you're feeling a sense of fear and uncertainty and discomfort—you've committed yourself to something that is much bigger and better than what you were doing before. Now you have to grow into it, and growth at the early stages doesn't feel very good." It lets them know that what they're experiencing is natural and not something to be avoided. It lets them know that fear isn't a sign that they should stop; rather, it's a step in the process toward a breakthrough. And this is something anyone can learn.

Indeed, The 4 C's Formula is the universal language for any person to grow into a bigger and better future.

Now, take 10 minutes to master the formula.
Before reading the rest of this small book, take the next 10 minutes to learn how The 4 C's Formula works. That's all it takes: 10 minutes to fundamentally transform how you're looking at your life.

Remember a growth experience. To make this easy, let's start with a personal growth experience from your past where you clearly went through the four growth stages of commitment, courage, capability, and confidence. This can be something that happened recently or from a long time ago—the only important criterion here is that you took a big jump in capability and confidence as a result of going through this experience.

Draw your own form. Using the example form on the opposite page, draw four boxes on a sheet of paper and label them in the same order: 1. Commitment, 2. Courage, 3. Capability, and 4. Confidence. You'll find that filling a whole page with the four boxes works best. At the top of the page, write down the name of the experience and the date when it happened.

Follow the formula. Recall your experience by writing down what your commitment to growth was in the situation.

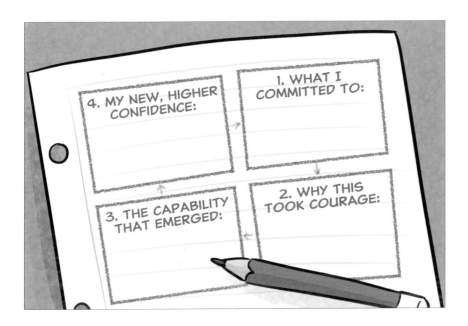

Then, describe the courage it required on your part to move forward on this commitment. Next, identify the new capability that emerged as a result of your courage. Finally, write down the new level of confidence you achieved from this whole experience.

Why it works. With your new 4 C's grasp of this past experience, you're ready to understand why this can now be the most important skill for the rest of your life. If possible, share what you've written with someone who you think will also benefit from using the formula. After you've thought about and discussed the process, keep it in mind as you read the rest of this book. Now that you've started using the formula, everything that follows will be much clearer.

Chapter 1:
Commitment Creates Courage

Commitment is the important first stage of The 4 C's Formula because without a strong, specific commitment, you might not have the motivation to even begin. Commitment happens when you make a sale—to yourself. It requires selling yourself on doing something you don't yet have the capability to pull off.

Everybody talks about sales in terms of selling to someone else, but, actually, the first sale that we have to make to advance our life forward is to sell ourselves on a goal. And the first part of making any sale is to intellectually engage yourself or someone else with a future desirable result.

In the commitment stage of the 4 C's process, you're stating a particular result. My own example is that, over the next 25 years, I've committed to creating 100 concepts that will be turned into 100 books—one per quarter. That is a measurable goal and it's measured quarter by quarter. This means that every time I start a brand new workshop quarter, I had better show up with a brand new concept and a brand new book.

Writing 100 books in 100 quarters.
When I made that commitment, I didn't yet have the capability of creating the result. Right now, with this second book, I have the capability of doing it twice. I don't have the capability of doing it 100 times. I know how I would go about it, but in order to keep doing it quarter after quarter, a lot of things need to happen, including making the process that we're creating here better and better. Otherwise, it will break down and we won't reach the goal.

That's what commitment requires you to do. It requires you

to improve communication and the methods you're using. The moment you commit, you might recognize that there is a large amount of the project you cannot pull off yourself. This immediately puts you in the courage stage, but you simply have to get as much assistance as you possibly can.

A commitment way beyond my capabilities.

I had committed to writing the book *Wanting What You Want*, but it was going to be a lot of hard work for me. Then, in early December, I was talking to my client and friend Dean Jackson, who created The 90-Minute Book process and whose team member Susan conducts interviews as the first step in producing small books for clients. During the course of the conversation, we decided that Susan would interview me on the subject of the book, and the 90-minute book that was produced would be the first draft toward the final version. That weekend, we started the process.

That was a huge jump for me because I had already committed to creating the 100 books, but I didn't yet have the capability. I had thought about doing this before, but I didn't have a committed deadline.

The moment I had the committed deadline, all of a sudden, I really had to scramble.

The specific commitment forced me into action. Then I realized that Kerri Morrison on my team could do part of it, and I just kept looking for more people to do their part. My own work that went into that book was the least amount of personal work of all the books I've written. I've never gotten away so easy. It all started as soon as the 90-minute book came back and Kerri responded to it with a commitment of her own.

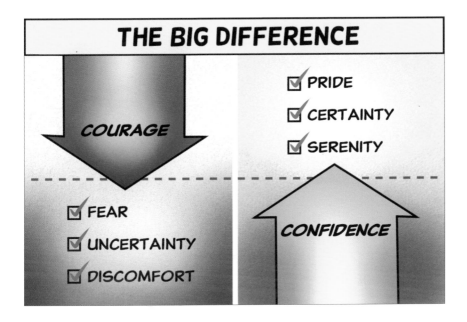

Procrastination stops; courage keeps going.

Often when we think of making a big commitment, we think of facing fear and uncertainty. Courage is your response to all those worries and fears, but the important thing is to keep going forward despite the temptation to procrastinate or to turn away from the commitment. The difference between procrastination and courage is that the procrastinator feels the fear and stops while the courageous person feels the fear and moves forward. Courage is a willingness to go forward in spite of not feeling confident. The opposite of courage isn't fear; it's cowardice. All of us experience fear, but we can respond to it in different ways.

Confidence feels good. Courage doesn't.

Courage doesn't feel very good, but that doesn't mean periods of courage aren't necessary or important. Whether it's a short period of courage or a long period of courage, we have to be completely okay with the fact that there is going to be a period of discomfort. It might last an hour. It might last a day. It might last a month.

In the process toward breakthrough results, we're going to go through a period where we feel a sense of fear, uncertainty, and anxiety, but this uncomfortable period is necessary if we're going to achieve increased capability and a higher level of confidence. If you're going to grow as an individual and an entrepreneur, you can't skip any of the steps. Courage is just as important as commitment, capability, or confidence.

My feeling is that courage must be talked about as a major skill and as a necessary step in the process of building confidence in any area.

Educators and coaches have to position it, saying, "Whenever you make a new commitment, before you get a new capability and the confidence that comes from it, you have to go through a period of courage."

Once courage is accepted as a normal and necessary step toward achieving goals, we'll see more and more people who are willing to go through that phase with the faith that on the other side are new capabilities and greater confidence.

There is a danger in letting people believe that requiring courage is weak and that going through a period of courage shouldn't be necessary. When individuals try to avoid those feelings of fear, this is where addiction comes in. A lot of people get their confidence through drug or alcohol abuse

or some other harmful activity. There is an appearance of confidence, but it's not a useful confidence. It's artificial.

Addictions start with a lack of confidence.

There's a significant level of addiction among entrepreneurs, including alcoholism, drug addiction, gambling, and especially workaholism. And these addictions generally start very early. For a lot of entrepreneurs, the addiction began in their teens. As a matter of fact, almost all addictions, with the exception of painkillers, start before age twenty.

I believe that what's behind addictions, especially starting in teenagers, is a lack of confidence. They want to grow. They know they have to grow. They know they have to get better. But they're not entirely committed to it, so they're caught in a no-man's land where they're feeling the fear, the uncertainty, and the discomfort but they don't have the capabilities to actually figure out what to do.

So instead they retreat into a behavior, whether it's drug abuse, alcohol abuse, or any other addictive behavior, and it makes them feel good for a while. It gives them the sense that they've regained control. The problem is that it's self-destructive in a number of ways. For one thing, they become very dependent upon their addiction. Moreover, the addiction merely gives the superficial appearance that they're confident and capable, but they don't feel that way inside—they haven't actually grown as human beings.

These dangerous activities can be avoided by making sure we talk about courage in response to fear as a natural step of human growth.

By taking away the negativity and stigma associated with fear and anxiety, and by clearly stating that courage, while uncomfortable, is worth persevering through, more and more people won't feel a need to avoid or delay this important stage and will instead gather their courage and push through toward major breakthroughs and achievements in their lives.

A commitment can be made right now.

Here's a final way of thinking about the difference between procrastination and commitment. Imagine building a new house where everything is perfectly designed and constructed—except you forget to install electricity. You move into the house, and something always seems "not quite perfect." So you keep adding to what already exists: landscaping, furniture, decorations, carpeting, etc. As time goes on, it's more and more of the same, but there's no energy or

power to make your house liveable.

This is what procrastination is like: It's the continual activity of trying to improve your life without the energy or power of commitment behind it because you're afraid of the courage that will be required the moment you commit. But just think of the experiences you've had every time you actually did start with commitment. Yes, the courage stage that followed was a bit scary, uncertain, and uncomfortable. But every time you allowed yourself to go through this process, you took a big jump. And you'll immediately take another big jump if you make a commitment right now.

Chapter 2:
Courage Creates Capability

When you commit to achieving a breakthrough in your per-formance and results, that commitment triggers the courage to go into unknown territory. Courage suddenly puts you in a position where you can fail, and it's scary because you're risking what you've already achieved. You're betting your past and present on your future. You're taking yourself out of your existing comfort zone, letting go of your existing confidence to create a higher level of confidence.

This puts your brain on high alert that it now has to create an entirely new capability. You get a big rush of adrenaline, your sense of urgency sharpens, and your mind simplifies your priorities and decisions. You eliminate all alternatives except success, and you are highly energized to make the breakthrough.

Long courage vs. short courage.
At the moment you make a commitment, you may not yet have the capability or confidence to pull it off, so when you go into action anyway and start moving toward the result, that takes courage. It doesn't mean you feel good about it, but you're going to persist until the new capability and confidence actually come into play. And while you might not have a choice about going through a period of courage, you do have a choice as to whether it's going to be a long period or a short period.

In my case, a long period of courage would have been com-mitting to creating the books and then thinking I had to do it all on my own. But if I did that, I would have been extending the courage period for months. Instead, the moment I made

the commitment and started experiencing fear, uncertainty, and discomfort, I thought of all the people, both on my team and outside of my team, who could be involved in the process. I realized that while the commitment I'd made was scary, I didn't have to do it all by myself.

The uncomfortable period of courage is also shortened by the strength of your commitment.

The more specific your goals and deadlines are, the stronger and more achievable your commitment will be.

And by writing it down, by putting that commitment down on paper, your resolve to get it done will be even stronger.

On the other hand, if you've only made a 75 percent commitment, your period of courage is going to be longer because you've short-changed it by 25 percent. Any degree of commitment less than 100 percent automatically extends the period of courage that's required. If you make a 50 percent commitment, you've doubled the amount of courage that's required because you haven't really set yourself up properly.

You've made yourself liable to something, but you haven't given yourself the resources you need to pull it off. You've put yourself in a situation where there can't be a good ending to what you're doing. It's vital never to obligate yourself to something you're not completely committed to.

Outside of existing capability and confidence.

Now, this is key: You can skip the courage step, but you won't turn out a result that is any better than what you've achieved before. You'll simply be operating within your

present level of capability and confidence.

Courage comes into play when you've comitted yourself to something outside your level of confidence and capability. It's the commitment without the guarantee of capability or confidence that scares you.

When I committed to creating 100 concepts and 100 books, I didn't know how I was going to pull it off because I'd never done anything like it before at that scale. I was putting myself outside of my area of confidence and capability. But there's an energy you gain when you make a commitment and enter a state of courage that quickly leads to capability.

What I've noticed over the years, after having coached more than 2,000 Strategic Coach workshops, is that I'm scared for about a half-hour before the workshop begins. I fear that I'm not going to do as well as I have before, that I'm going to go backward. But what I say to myself is, since I'm going through the bother of being scared, I might as well turn the fear into something new.

Don't get caught between "dock" and "boat."

Even if you think you have everything handled and you're at the top of your game, the world isn't going to stay the same. You may be confronted with all sorts of crises that require even more painful and scary changes in your life. And while most people are forced into growth and change by circumstances outside of their control, what entrepreneurs do is voluntarily scare themselves into growth.

We have all sorts of situations in life where people get a notion that something bigger and better is needed in their life and voluntarily make a change, where others have to be compelled. The ones who voluntarily do it are always enormously more successful than the ones who don't because it becomes a skill: They have this skill of continually self-initiating their own growth.

Say, for example, you want to take a boat ride, but you're afraid to leave the dock. You have one foot in the boat and the other on the dock. When you untie the boat and let it drift out into the water, you're making a commitment. Those who have not made the commitment, on the other hand, are still keeping one foot on the dock. In some ways, they are in the worst of both worlds. A part of them wants to go on a boat ride, the other one wants to stay on the dock, and they refuse to make a decision.

What happens when you make the commitment is that you're saying, to a certain extent:

"I'm going to put at risk everything I already know and have already created because I want a payoff that is much bigger."

But in order to do that, you have to relinquish for a period of time that sense of security you had before and go into a state where you're experiencing fear and uncertainty.

Only then will your brain invent an entirely new way of doing something you couldn't see before. Once you voluntarily give up the security and confidence you had before and are willing to go through a period of being fearful and uncertain, your creative brain will assemble all your experiences and pull together all sorts of possibilities to create a new capability. With that new capability, you're going to achieve a bigger and better result, which will ultimately lead to an increase in confidence.

Where and why all innovation is triggered.

I believe that all innovation starts when people are thrown into situations where they have to be committed to getting a bigger and better result. It could be that they lost their job, their business collapsed, the market changed, or they voluntarily put themselves in that position. Whatever the case may be, once there, they get entirely new ideas. They see entirely new possibilities and solutions they never saw before. That's where the new capability comes through.

You cannot sit on the sidelines and try to come up with a new capability. You have to actually be in the stress of the situation, and then you'll work your way out of it.

You have to let go of the dock. You have to let go of the security you've built up from all your previous achievements and say, "I'm putting myself back in the starting position."

A lot of people, when they get really successful, have so much invested in their prior success that the notion of putting it at risk is anathema. This is one of the pitfalls of being successful.

Everything falls away except your Unique Ability.

But one of the great things that happens when you let yourself go through the uncomfortable period of courage is that you naturally zero in on your most powerful areas of unique skill and passion. In Strategic Coach, we call this being in your Unique Ability, which is where your greatest energy,

usefulness, and creativity are always found.

Being in a committed state of courage enables you to use your Unique Ability to innovate entirely new, unpredictable capabilities.

I mentioned earlier that when creating the book *Wanting What You Want*, I got away with doing the least amount of work I'd ever done on one of my books. What I was really doing was focusing only on the part I love to do and do best and letting the team around me use their own areas of Unique Ability to complete the project.

In the courage phase of the 4 C's process, everything but your Unique Ability falls away, setting you up to be your most innovative and creative.

Chapter 3:
Capability Creates Confidence

The activity of going through a period of courage—with a clear breakthrough commitment in mind—produces the innovative energy to create a new, more powerful capability. And the moment you acquire this capability, your confidence takes a big jump.

Cathy Davis, who I talked about earlier, had to make a commitment and had to go through her courageous first day in the video studio to create a new presentation capability. Armed with this new capability, she walked into the studio on the second day with a much higher level of confidence. In two days, she created a breakthrough in both her performance and results.

Ever-increasing confidence creates 100 books.
For me, getting the the original "90-minute book" back from Susan Austin (thanks to Dean Jackson) as the first step in producing the first of 100 books was a major capability that gave me a great amount of confidence. It reassured me that I had the resources to create these little books and that I had something tangible to give to Kerri Morrison to complete the next stage of the process.

Kerri herself went through the 4 C's process in creating *Wanting What You Want*. When I first approached her with a copy of the 90-minute book and the proposal that she take that copy and organize it and edit it into a final version of the book, she immediately committed to doing it. Only later did she tell me that she went through her own period of courage in taking on the task.

In my previous book writing process, Kerri would come in toward the end to edit the final copy. She didn't yet have

the capability—or the confidence that follows—of being involved in such an early stage of the writing process. But having made the commitment, she dove in and completed the task at hand.

She submitted her copy to me and, as she admitted to me later, waited anxiously for my reply. When I got back to her the following day and let her know how happy I was with her work, she was just soaring for the rest of that month. By committing to the task and getting it done despite her fear, she came through the other side with a new capability. She really grew by going through this process, and the confidence that resulted from the new capability made her excited to get to work on the next book, the one you're reading now.

Bigger futures come from new capabilities.

Confidence is the by-product of gaining a new capability. When people are looking for a bigger and better future, it's really that they're looking to gain the capability of doing something better and producing bigger results.

There's a wide spectrum of different capabilities—personal capability, team capability, funding capability—but essentially what having a new capability means is that you can get something done in the future that you can't get done now, or you can get something done in the future in a far better way than you're doing it now.

Confidence is how you feel as a result of acquiring the capability. That confidence, in turn, creates the capability to make a bigger commitment.

Each of the 4 C's represents a different kind of experience that actually sets up the next one. Commitment is a particular type of experience that sets up the possibility of the experience of courage. Courage is a particular type of experience that sets up the possibility of capability. Capability is a particular type of experience that sets up the possibility of confidence. Then it repeats itself.

New capabilities also change your past.
New capability creates confidence ahead of it, but it also rearranges everything behind it. Any jump in capability automatically transforms both the past and the future. Most successful people are comfortable with the idea that they create and change their future by imagining and achieving their bigger goals, but what most people never think about is that every new breakthrough in their capabilities and con-

fidence also immediately changes the meaning and usefulness of their past experiences.

Here's an example of this: My three best capabilities are asking thought-provoking questions, drawing pictures of people's answers to my questions, and then turning their diagrammed answers into new questions that are useful to both them and me.

The more that I've become successful as an entrepreneur with these three skills, and the more I am rewarded for my success, the more I can understand my life before I became an entrepreneur, in the period from 1944 to 1974, and the clearer I get about my breakthroughs and growth over the past 40 years.

But the deeper reality of my growth over my entire life really lies in all of my 4 C's experiences. Every time I have gone through the process of commitment, courage, capability, and confidence, I have taken a big jump in my performance and results. This was true when I was ten years old, when I was forty, and now that I am over seventy. The single structure and process that knits my whole life together going both backward and forward is always The 4 C's Formula.

Greater confidence is always its own reward.

There are a lot of rewards when you acquire a new capability. One is that your contribution is automatically bigger. Especially when you're in a team situation, immediately your contribution to your teamwork goes way up. As well, your respect, admiration, and appreciation for everybody else in your organization increases.

ENDLESS EXPANSION

But the biggest reward from going through the first three stages of commitment, courage, and capability is greater confidence. And greater confidence is its own reward. The truth is that everyone, in everything they do on a daily basis, is striving for greater confidence. Everyone loves the feeling of confidence: the sense of certainty and serenity that makes everything feel "right." In our daydreams and fantasies, we wish we could always feel this way. These good feelings in the moment, however, are actually just part of the reward.

The bigger payoff from achieving greater confidence is actually a much stronger motivation and ability to start The 4 C's Formula all over again at a much higher level of performance and impact. And to keep doing this for the rest of your life.

Chapter 4:
Confidence Creates (More) Commitment

People who increase their confidence have the advantage of being able to make bigger commitments—which lead to bigger breakthroughs. Over and over again.

I've seen this with my entrepreneurial clients, I've seen this in my own life, and I've seen it with my team members at Strategic Coach. Once Cathy Davis had gained her new capability in the studio, she couldn't wait to make even bigger commitments to creating new videos and doing it faster, easier, and better than she had previously. Once Kerri Morrison had gained her new capability and role in the book-writing process, she was excited and eager to get started on the next book.

Confidence can also create complacency.

But confidence can also create complacency. Because confidence feels so good, there's a temptation to stay in this stage. You might have persistent thoughts like, "But, I like it here." "It's so comfortable." "Why can't it last?" "I've worked so hard to get here!"

If you don't get back into the game right away, though, with a higher level of commitment, the confidence you've gained from your last jump in capability will start to erode. After a while, you start to doubt all your previous achievements.

The only way to solidify the present level of confidence that you've achieved through the 4 C's process is by making a bigger commitment that puts this confidence at risk.

All of the positive and energizing feelings of confidence have

an expiry date on them. You can enjoy them and luxuriate in that stage for a while, but then you have to get back into the 4 C's game. Once the reward period is over and you've acknowledged and celebrated your achievements, it's time to make a bigger commitment to an even bigger break-through. It's time to gain a capability that's larger than what you've just achieved.

And this new level of confidence you have from your most recent achievement means you're capable of committing to a higher level of capability.

Flexing your courage muscles at a higher level.

The 4 C's Formula repeats endlessly, always leading to higher and higher levels of capability and confidence. And of course these higher levels of capability and confidence require bigger commitments and more courage.

It's crucial to keep flexing and strengthening our 4 C's mus-cles: Commitment muscles, Courage muscles, Capability muscles, and Confidence muscles. After all, no one could expect to stay in top physical shape without constant exer-cise and bigger challenges.

Just like increasing intensity with exercise, you flex your courage muscles and always look for more resistance and a bigger challenge every time you make a new commitment. You can say to yourself, "I was able to handle this much fear last time, and I think I can handle more fear this time."

I believe that once we get good at one level, we natu-rally and automatically test ourselves to see if we can go even higher.

CAPABILITIES EMERGE WHEN YOU *RISK YOUR CONFIDENCE.*

This formula helps you to push the envelope in terms of commitment, push the envelope to be more courageous, push the envelope to create a bigger and better capability, and push the envelope in becoming more confident than ever before.

It's a closed loop system. Every new 4 C's experience gives you extra impetus to raise the bar the next time you go through the cycle.

Creating many different kinds of capabilities.

With each new commitment, there are lots of other capabilities that you also want to acquire at the same time. It's very seldom that your whole life is dependent upon one future capability. Some of these capabilities are personal, some of them are organizational. In the 21st century, more and more of them involve teamwork. And all of them need to be balanced with one another so that as you're growing, you're also enjoying an integrated life with an increasing sense of meaning.

The best way to look at this balance of capabilities is to think about the stock market. One of the wisdoms about the stock market is that it's important to have a balanced portfolio. You don't put all of your capital in one investment.

The same is true with capabilities. We tend to treat our personal, teamwork, and organizational future like a mutual fund. We're balancing improvements and several other capabilities all the time. Each of them requires a risk, but none of them should require a total risk.

As we grow through the 4 C's process, we develop many different kinds of capabilities that enable us to live and enjoy an increasingly balanced life. Each of these capabilities came about because we were willing to risk our existing level of confidence to create something new.

Achieving through 90-day breakthroughs.

At any given time, you have a finite amount of courage for for that period. For example, over the next 90 days, I have a finite amount of courage to make use of. The question is, what is the best focus for my courage? The immediate answer is that I want to focus on things that have the biggest possible payoff and on things that, once I achieve them, will continue to multiply in value.

In my everyday life, because I have a finite amount of courage to invest in creating higher capabilities, I plan to do just three important things a day. But having a limited amount

of courage makes me so much more strategic about what I invest in. It also means that the goals I choose to set for myself are ones that I am 100 percent committed to and ones that align with my values and my purpose.

The 4 C's continually develops many different kinds of surprising capabilities in entirely new areas of our lives. This is why it will always be exciting to start again on the 4 C's process at a higher level. When you make a new commitment, you don't know what new capabilities will be created.

From start to finish, The 4 C's Formula is always predictable in its structure—which is reassuring. But at the same time, the formula is always innovative in its process and surprising in its outcomes—which is exciting.

Chapter 5:
You're The Chief Commitment Officer

As the leader of your company, you are always the role model for practicing the 4 C's—starting with commitment. That makes you the "Chief Commitment Officer." When you commit to something 100 percent, it encourages everybody else to do the same. This simplifies what leadership is always about: continually making commitment, courage, capability, and confidence the fundamental philosophy, structure, and process for all progress and growth in your company.

Achieving through 90-day breakthroughs.
Being the first to commit puts you in the lead. It then puts you in the spotlight with everyone on your team watching your courage. Now everybody else will be motivated to break out of their comfort zones. The moment this happens, your whole company breaks through to new levels of capability and confidence.

When I made the commitment to create 100 books in 100 quarters, one of the things that lessened the fear factor that came from that was determining that I was just one member of a team. I wasn't carrying the commitment entirely on my shoulders. By involving a team of people, I spread out the risk. And I spread it out on the basis of other people's areas of Unique Ability.

In my role as owner and leader of my organization, I could just focus on the one thing that would have a huge multiplier effect—developing brand new concepts—and then build a unified team that could actually pull off the result—100 new books. In this way, my entire leadership role in the company, my role as Chief Commitment Officer, was taken to a higher level.

No escaping it—you're the "CCO."

When I publicly make a big commitment to a big goal, it leads the rest of the team to ask themselves, "If Dan can commit himself to that, what can I commit myself to?" The Chief Commitment Officer leads the way. You devote yourself to a commitment that is so powerful, it inspires everybody else to make their own commitments and go through their own periods of courage.

Entrepreneurs are always the Chief Commitment Officers in their companies. There's no avoiding this. You may fail at it—if you're not committing, then you're the chief commitment *preventer*. But whether you're the chief catalyst for commitment in your office or the chief preventer of commitment, you're the CCO and people will look to you.

Nobody else can make a commitment if you're not committing. People are expecting it of you. They're not going to move unless you move. Nobody's going to take a risk unless you take a risk.

Being the Chief Commitment Officer is the number-one role of an entrepreneur in any company. You're the one who has the picture of the future, and you're the only one who can initiate an action that requires courage for the whole company. Your team is inspired by your demonstration of commitment and your being willing to risk your current level of confidence to get to a new level of capability.

What's necessary for you as the Chief Commitment Officer is to stop involving yourself in activities that don't require commitment. As the entrepreneurial owner of a company, you shouldn't be involved in any area of activity where there isn't an improvement in each of the 4 C's.

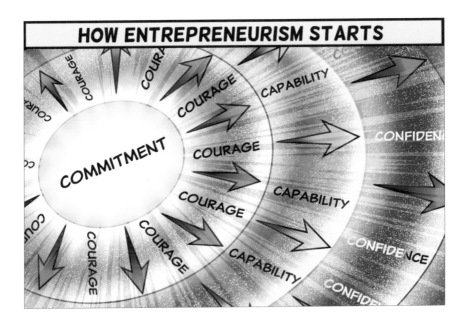

HOW ENTREPRENEURISM STARTS

COMMITMENT

COURAGE

CAPABILITY

CONFIDENCE

Indeed, entrepreneurs are only entrepreneurs when they're involved in the 4 C's process. If they're not, then they're on autopilot, and this is where organizations start to deteriorate. The energy goes out of the company when the team perceives that the leader is on autopilot.

If the owner is not making commitments, not going through the stages of courage, capability, and confidence, then the team isn't either. It's as though somebody turned off the electricity. You've got all the machinery of the organization, but somebody switched off the power.

It's the 4 C's activity that, like a generator, supplies all the electricity of an organization. As an entrepreneur, as an owner, you're the one who turns on the switch.

Chapter 6:
Courage Multiplies Leadership

Shortly after President John F. Kennedy was elected in 1960, he declared that by the end of the decade, the United States would put a man on the moon and bring him back safely to Earth.

The only problem was, they didn't have the foggiest idea how to do that.

They didn't have any of the technology at the time to get astronauts to the moon and get them back safely. They had the capability to send rockets up 20 miles, but sending a man to the moon was a completely different thing. They didn't know how they were going to create the space module. They didn't know how to keep people alive in space for a successful roundtrip voyage to the moon. But Kennedy committed to the goal.

Then they beat the deadline by a year.

Leadership grows out of demonstrated courage.
We always remember the greatest leaders as people who make commitments and put themselves in a position where they could be seen as complete failures. In other words, they are taking a risk with their existing reputation.

In this book, I am focusing specifically on leadership in the entrepreneurial world. The 4 C's Formula sorts out who the leaders are in any business in any industry. They are the people who make a commitment and are willing to go for it, both for themselves and also for their organization. As a result, other people can organize their activities to support the commitment that the entrepreneurial leader has made.

When people say they admire leadership, they're actually saying they value courage, because leaders are those who are willing to go into uncharted territory. They're willing to take a risk without a guarantee of success.

Those who own their own businesses are automatically leaders in the eyes of those around them—their teams, clientele, suppliers, and families. But owning something in the present only says that you had courage in the past. It doesn't say that you're a leader. Something else is required, and that's the constant practice of being courageous in relation to the future. If you continually strengthen this one activity, your reputation as a leader will always multiply in everyone's eyes.

The people we perceive as being really powerful leaders are those who made commitments and then demonstrated the courage to get to a new level of capability and confidence. This is natural leadership. Anybody can be a leader by following this framework. You are a leader whenever you apply the 4 C's to any situation.

Courage is the universal proof of growth.

It's important for leaders to be open and straightforward if they want commitment and courage to be contagious in their organizations. There's an enormous amount of wasted opportunity in life simply because people want to show only their capability and confidence. If you look at the effectiveness of programs like the 12-step program for people with addictions, the power of the program, and the reason people keep showing up for the meetings and will stay sober for another day, another week, another month, is because when they go to the meetings, they're in the presence of

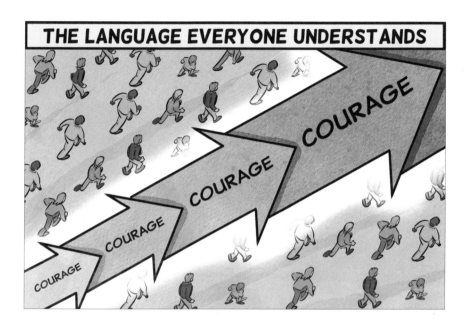

people who are sharing their commitment and their courage.

Nothing gives us a sense of solidarity like sharing our commitment and courage. Capability and confidence don't give us solidarity. They're the rewards for making commitments and having courage.

The first two stages of the 4 C's are where we can connect, where we can relate to people, where we can empathize. Those stages, and the entire 4 C's Formula, are universal, and when we're open about our experiences, even when we're feeling fear, we let others know that these stages are normal and that even great leaders go through periods of uncertainty and discomfort.

As human beings, we think we're going to be admired for our

capability and confidence, and we strive to hide our commitment and courage. But what's really meaningful and valuable to human beings isn't the payoff—it's the process we all go through. It's the knowledge of a shared experience.

You're really at your most understandable as a human being in the commitment and courage stages, not in the capability and confidence stages. A lot of leaders think that part of their role is to not show that they're going through periods of risk and courage because they think it's a weakness and a failure. But that's a mistake. We all want to grow, and courage is the proof that we are succeeding.

In a context where people have the 4 C's as a common language, courage is seen as a necessary part of a bigger process and not something to hide.

In the case of JFK, he took a really big risk, but the day after he made his commitment, suddenly the space program was radically different. People saw that the President was staking the reputation of the country on this. He was willing to stake his own political reputation on it. His commitment and courage catalyzed everybody else to make a deeper commitment and to go into their own states of courage.

Your courage immediately inspires everyone.

Great leadership stories share a common structure: A massive commitment was made that required extraordinary courage, but then immediately the commitment and courage were distributed throughout the group.

Every time one person demonstrates personal courage, it immediately becomes possible for a lot of people to take

risks with new ideas and new processes. In the entrepreneurial world, this is how new innovations become successful breakthroughs in the marketplace. The innovator's courage creates a powerful and contagious situation where new capabilities and confidence can be acquired by many other individuals.

Because of The 4 C's Formula, which is a system of thinking, communication, and action that always produces bigger capabilities and higher confidence, you can see that courage is something to be welcomed, embraced, and taken advantage of as often as possible in everyday life. This is what leadership is for everyone on the planet, and showing courage is something that everyone on the planet can do.

Chapter 7:
Where All Innovation Starts

If you're using The 4 C's Formula as an ongoing process for your business, innovation is automatically built in.

Innovation occurs in the dynamic thinking zone between courage and capability. The moment you risk your past and present for the sake of a bigger and better future breakthrough, your brain instantly becomes creative, innovative, and inventive.

Between courage and capability, you put yourself in a position where you have no alternative except to create something new, bigger, and better. That's innovation. It's not about being clever. It's about being courageous.

One of the great breakthroughs in history was when human beings learned how to create electrical charges and then capture the charge and channel its energy. What they discovered is that you have to create a differential between a negative and a positive. That's when you get a spark.

Likewise, when you commit to creating a larger capability, you're creating a differential in your mind between your existing capability and a future capability—generating a spark of creativity and innovation.

Your brain accelerates in response to risk.

Because you were totally confident about your existing capability, and you're not confident at all about the future capability, you're immediately put into a state of courage.

But you're not coming into that situation without resources. You have an enormous amount of experience to draw from, which, unless you put yourself in a state of courage, you

WHERE ALL INNOVATION IS CREATED
3
CAPABILITY
2
COURAGE
EXPERIENCE
INNOVATION
YIKES!
INNOVATION REQUIRES FEAR & EXCITEMENT
WOW!

couldn't access. The state of courage catalyzes your previous experience, and your mind immediately starts looking for any previous situation where you pulled off something like this.

You start putting experiences together very rapidly, and it's that rapid catalyzing of all your experiences, and then the experiences of people on your team, that suggests to you that there's an entirely new way to do this.

Innovation is the electricity that's generated from the stress and the strain between a future situation you've committed yourself to and not yet having the capability to achieve it.

Innovation creates your independent future.

Innovation isn't possible without risk. You have to be willing to give up what you already have for the chance of gaining something better.

When circumstances change in your life—say a new innovation takes place—it can either be a bad thing or a good thing depending on whether you believe that you can create a higher level of capability in response to the new situation.

I'm not afraid of a lot of changes in the world because I know I can always bump my capability up to take care of the new circumstances. I have a commitment to growing, responding, being creative, and being a leader.

And if you're committed to being a leader, and to always increasing your capability, other people's innovations aren't a threat, even if they change how things are currently hap-

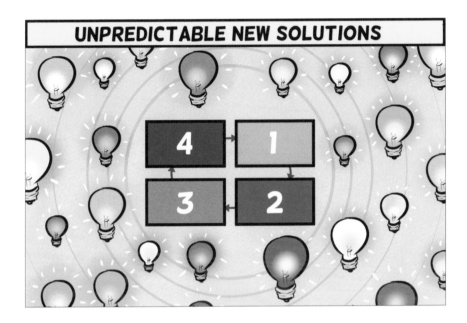

pening. When you are innovative yourself, you are also increasingly interested in what other innovative entrepreneurs are doing. When innovation becomes a normal and continual activity for you and your company, then operating in a world of unpredictable innovations becomes exciting rather than a threatening experience.

If I practice the 4 C's on a daily basis, I don't have to worry about what's coming next, how the world's going to change, or the challenges the company's going to face, because I know I have a way of coming to grips with that. I know I am always going to be innovating in an innovative world involving millions of other entrepreneurs and their teams. I know that I'm going to handle anything that happens in the future the way I handled everything in the past. That is, I'm going to take my capability to a higher level.

Chapter 8:
Remembering Your 4 C's Wins

By understanding The 4 C's Formula, you'll recognize how you became successful. Your previous entrepreneurial breakthroughs happened because of commitment, courage, capability, and confidence. Every time you followed this process, you achieved a big win. Your biggest progress and past achievements have always been the result of following the formula.

Many entrepreneurs don't like thinking about the past because they are future-focused. That usually makes sense. But there is one area of your past that will always be worth identifying, studying, learning from, and bringing along into your future: Every time you followed The 4 C's Formula, you created a breakthrough. It's that simple. It's that valuable. And every one of your 4 C's wins is worth remembering.

Each time you made a commitment before you had the capability and confidence, and were willing to go through a period of courage, it was one of the most important building blocks you had in your life and career.

Designing a future requiring even more courage.
Some people will tell you a wonderful story about their past, having made all these breakthroughs, and they'll agree that they went through the 4 C's to achieve them. But then they'll try to design a future where courage is no longer required. But if you avoid going through periods of courage, you won't have any more breakthroughs.

For the rest of your life, as a growing entrepreneur, you're going to have to go through all four stages, and the most important one that's going to really make the difference,

that's going to create the breakthrough, is the willingness to go through a period of courage.

Living a life without courage just doesn't work. You want more capability and confidence, but you have to pay with commitment and courage.

Really successful entrepreneurs, individuals who continually grow and make jumps in their businesses, have mastered this four-stage process. But in every case, when they made a new commitment, they had to go through that period of courage. Even though they were successful and accomplished and had tremendous capability, when they committed themselves to a new breakthrough, they had to go through a period of courage again.

A future of always bigger breakthroughs.

You've reached your present level of success as the result of dozens and probably hundreds of breakthroughs, both personal and organizational, big and small. In order to have a future that's even more successful than what you've already achieved, it's crucial to think in terms of even more breakthroughs that are bigger and better than everything you've achieved in the past.

And the only way you can do this is by operating within The 4 C's Formula as your normal, everyday approach for the rest of your life.

The 4 C's are enjoyable if you do them quickly.

If you understand the 4 C's process, you'll see that it's not an onerous activity. It's actually an enjoyable process. You don't stay in any one of the 4 C's stages forever. You only

stay in the commitment stage long enough to create the courage stage. You only stay in the courage stage long enough to create the capability. And you only stay in the capability stage long enough to create that next level of confidence. Each stage is crucially important, but you're not to stay in any one of them longer than is necessary.

The next time you go through a period of courage, you'll be conscious of what you're looking for—a new capability that's going to produce the result. The moment you start getting the capability, your confidence is going to build.

It isn't as though you'll be in a state of courage until you get the confidence. You'll be in a state of courage only until you can start seeing the new capability developing, and then the confidence comes quickly.

Your growing skill of going through the whole process, over and over again, is what's key here and one of the most important skills you can master during your entire life, both as an individual and as an entrepreneur. Master the 4 C's, and you'll find yourself mastering hundreds of other skills as well.

How to electrify entrepreneurial discussions.

You can simplify your past by determining that the only value to you in your entrepreneurial career are the times you went through this 4 C's process. Sit down for a couple of hours and you could probably identify 100 situations—small, medium, and large—where you did this, and every time you did it, you took a jump.

By looking at how you got where you are and remembering the best of yourself, you gain confidence for the future. I can only have the best of me in the future to the degree that I appreciate the best of me in the past. Having these two understandings dictates what my present behavior is too. It's really hard to have a bigger and better future if you don't create a bigger and better past.

As I mentioned, I ask the participants in my workshops to choose an experience from their past and map it out according to The 4 C's Formula. It takes them about ten minutes. The atmosphere in the room is just electric after this because they have not only discovered an explanation for how they achieved success in this past experience, they immediately realize that this is all they have to do to achieve greater success in the future.

It had been something that was very hazy and murky and

YOUR 4 C'S PAST = YOUR 4 C'S FUTURE

disconnected and disorganized, and all of a sudden, their entire entrepreneurial past clarifies. They see exactly what they could do with the future and the present. They know exactly what they should be doing today, tomorrow, and the next day.

You can clearly see that the most memorable parts of your entrepreneurial career are the periods of courage where you made a commitment without evidence or proof that it would pay off. It was the courage parts of your past that produced the jumps in your entrepreneurial life and those things you're most proud of. You know that thinking and operating this way has always worked. And you know that now, with the 4 C's as your formula, it will work even better in the future.

Vision:
Past, Present, And Future 4 C's

Commitment, courage, capability, and confidence—if everything you and your entrepreneurial team do is based on these four strengths, everything your company does will produce the best possible performance, results, and reputation. As the world gets more complicated, you can simplify everything in your entrepreneurial life with The 4 C's Formula.

What the 4 C's does is take people who are achievers and who naturally succeed and give them the formula and language for how they do what they do. It takes the natural way that all growth happens and makes it conscious. It makes it systematic. It makes it shareable. It makes it so that people can learn from it.

Advantage of committing to 10x breakthroughs.

Entrepreneurs who have 10x ambitions know that in stating a 10x higher goal, they're lacking, right now, the capability to actually get there. A 10x goal automatically guarantees that in the present, you don't yet have the capabilities to achieve it.

Because of that, any statement of a 10x breakthrough puts you in a situation where it's going to require an extraordinary amount of commitment and courage to get there. The very nature of the game guarantees that it's going to require courage, and the primary commitment and courage are going to have to come from you as the entrepreneurial owner of your company.

As well, your commitments and courage have to be shared with your organization. By communicating this with your team, you spread the risk associated with the commitment to

everybody else in the company. But you're not asking anyone on your team to make a commitment or have courage beyond what's necessary for each of them to contribute.

This instantly propels your organization to become a 4 C's organization. It also forces people to choose whether they want to be a part of that. Those who embrace the 4 C's model are committed to growth, can make commitments, know they can count on themselves and teamwork to make that happen, and are willing to experience that uncomfortable period of courage.

You have your 4 C's and they have theirs.

By sharing the 10x breakthroughs and being transparent, you allow other people to step up. You attract the right kind of people who are engaged in that process and want it, and it will repel those who aren't willing to fly at that level.

The question I ask myself is, what do I want my team to be engaged with? The answer is that I want everybody in Strategic Coach to be engaged in the 4 C's process for themselves.

If they're engaged in their own 4 C's process in their daily activities, that level of engagement will produce the results they want, and it will produce the best results for the company as a whole.

I'm not asking anyone on my team to be engaged in my 4 C's Formula. I'm asking them to be engaged in their own. It's about having them aligned with that process, speaking the same language, so that, together, we can do great things and grow. Indeed, The 4 C's Formula is a universal

language of human growth. It takes only ten minutes for anyone to understand it, and it takes less than 30 minutes of practice to make it a permanent skill.

Creating a Self-Multiplying Company.

Everybody who makes a commitment inside of a team situation really wants their commitment to be resonant and congruent with everybody else's commitments. Everybody who's courageous in a team situation wants their courage to be useful to other people. They want their courage to be supportive of other people's courage and vice versa. That creates a very powerful, continual environment of innovation and of new capabilities.

What happens when you have that widely shared commitment and courage is that you get payoffs in terms of capability that always exceed what the commitment originally envisioned. You immediately get a huge boost of confidence, which raises you to the next level where you can make even bigger commitments.

In this way, your organization becomes a Self-Multiplying Company. It happens one person at a time, but there is a contagious, viral effect to the 4 C's where it begins to spread. It removes a lot of theory from life—there's nothing theoretical about the 4 C's. It's ultimately just practice. It removes abstractions, and things become very practical and tangible.

It's not about making a general commitment. It has to be a specific commitment. It's not about a general sort of courage. It has to be a specific courage. Our brains don't respond to generalities. Everything must be specific. When human beings operate in an environment where everything is specific, it brings an enormous level of reality.

It's the numbers and the deadlines that make a commitment. Otherwise, it's just a wish. It's just a slogan.

The miracle happens after full commitment.
For a lot of people, the reason their lives don't move forward is that they're never thinking and talking about the future in such a way that there is actually a commitment to a different kind of result than what they're experiencing right now.

And the reason they won't make these bigger commitments is that they haven't been guaranteed the capability and the confidence to do it. But that's not the way it works. Commitment and courage must come first, and it's those

who are willing to make those commitments, to take those risks, who gain the greatest capabilities and ultimately the confidence to keep making bigger breakthroughs.

In the story of the exodus from Egypt, the Bible recounts how the Hebrews arrived at the Red Sea, God parted the water, and they were able to cross safely and escape their enemies.

But the Jewish interpretation of this story states that the Red Sea didn't actually part and allow the people to cross until one of the tribe leaders, Nachshon, walked into the water up to his nose.

God just wanted to see a little commitment first.

The Strategic Coach Program
Expanding Entrepreneurial Freedom

The Strategic Coach Program, launched in 1989, has qualifications, measurements, structures, and processes that attract a particular type of talented, successful, and ambitious entrepreneur.

One differentiating quality of these Strategic Coach participants is that they recognize that the technology-empowered 21st century is a unique time to be an entrepreneur. It's the first time that a growing number of individuals with no special birth privileges and no special education can achieve almost anything they set their minds to.

These self-motivated individuals who participate in the three levels of Strategic Coach accept that if they can focus on mastering the right mindsets, they can experience increasing breakthroughs for themselves, both personally and professionally, that are new in history.

The 4 C's Formula is one of these breakthrough mindsets, and there are dozens more for you to master.

Mindsets that enable entrepreneurs to escape.
Many entrepreneurs have the potential and the willingness to achieve exponential goals in the 21st century, but they are blocked from taking action and making progress because they feel trapped in three ways:

• **Trapped thinking:** They are isolated by their own disconnected creativity, which continually churns out ideas that don't translate into achievement. *At Strategic Coach, entrepreneurs increasingly liberate their thinking to create entirely new practical breakthroughs for themselves and others.*

• **Trapped circumstances:** They are surrounded by people who don't support their ambitions, who actively oppose them, or who try to make them feel guilty about their achievements and dreams. *At Strategic Coach, entrepreneurs learn how to increasingly surround themselves with like-minded and like-motivated individuals in every area of their personal and business lives.*

• **Trapped energy:** They're using much of their daily energy to simply sustain themselves without ever actually experiencing exponential performance and results. They wanted to create a growing business but it turns out that they've only created a job—one that always stays the same. *At Strategic Coach, entrepreneurs continually transform every part of their business organizations so that they become self-managing, and then self-multiplying.*

Mindsets that enable entrepreneurs to achieve.
Around the world, the vast majority of entrepreneurs never get out of these trapped circumstances, but at Strategic Coach, our participants not only escape from these limitations, they also jump to extraordinary levels of achievement, success, and satisfaction.

They never stop growing. Strategic Coach participants continually transform how they think, how they make decisions, how they communicate, and how they take action based on their mastery of dozens of unique entrepreneurial mindsets that have been developed in the Program. These are purely entrepreneurial mindsets, like The 4 C's Formula.

We've taken a look at what goes on in the minds of the best entrepreneurs and have created a thinking system that is custom-designed for them and adjusts to the ambition of each individual.

The Strategic Coach Program provides an accelerating lifetime structure, process, and community for these entrepreneurs to create exponential breakthroughs.

Mindsets that enable entrepreneurs to multiply.

Depending on where you are right now in your life and business, we have a complete set of entrepreneurial mindsets that will immediately jump you up to the next level in terms of your ambition, achievements, and progress. Over the course of your entrepreneurial lifetime, you can move upward through our three levels of mindset measurement and scoring:

1. The Strategic Coach Signature Program: From isolation to teamwork. At this first breakthrough level, you create a Unique Ability Team that allows you to have a Self-Managing Company. Every successful entrepreneur dreams about having this kind of teamwork and this kind of organization. Through the Signature level of the Program, these dreams become a reality. In Strategic Coach, the Self-Managing Company is a practical growth system, not a motivational slogan.

2. The 10x Ambition Program: From teamwork to exponential. You make breakthroughs that transform your life, and your organization becomes a Self-Multiplying Company. Talented entrepreneurs want to free their biggest growth plans from non-supportive relationships, situations, and circumstances. Through the 10x Ambition level of Strategic Coach, their biggest aspirations attract multiplier capabilities, resources, and opportunities.

3. The Game Changer Program: From exponential to transformative. As your entrepreneurial life becomes exponential, your Self-Multiplying Company become transformative. *The key evidence of this is that your biggest competitors want to become your best students, customers, and promoters.* Game Changer entrepreneurs in Strategic Coach become the leading innovators and cutting-edge teachers in their industries and continually introduce new strategies, methods, and systems that create *new* industries.

Measure yourself, score yourself, get started.

The back cover of this book folds out into an Ambition Scorecard that enables you to score yourself according to eight unique Strategic Coach mindsets. Read through the four statements for each mindset and give yourself a score of 1 to 12 based on where your own mindset falls on the spectrum. Put each mindset's score in the first column at the right, and then add up all eight and put the total at the bottom. Now, think back ten years and identify the score you would have given yourself then for each of the mindsets. Write these in the "Past" column, add them up, and write in the total.

When you compare the two scores, you can see where you are in terms of your achievements and ambitions. If this fast exercise tells you that you want to multiply in all these areas, contact us today to get started:

The Strategic Coach Program is ready for you! Visit us online at *strategiccoach.com* or call us at 416.531.7399 or 1.800.387.3206.

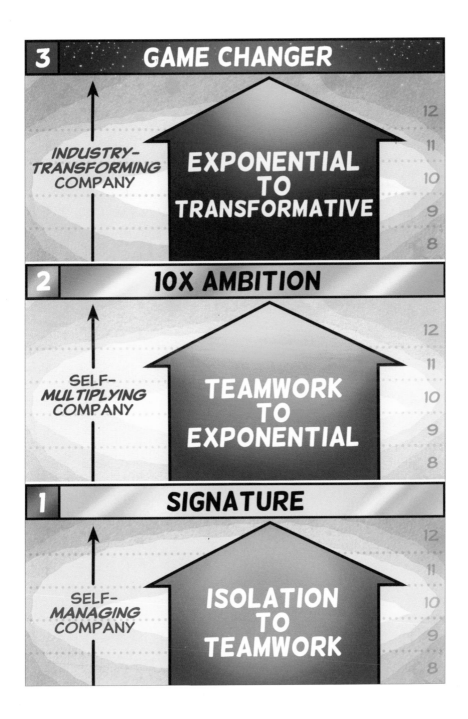

About The Author
Dan Sullivan

 Dan Sullivan is the founder and president of The Strategic Coach Inc. and creator of the Strategic Coach® Program, which helps accomplished entrepreneurs reach new heights of success and happiness. He has over 40 years of experience as a strategic planner and coach to entrepreneurial individuals and groups. He is author of over 30 publications, including *The Great Crossover, The 21st Century Agent, Creative Destruction, How The Best Get Better®,* and *Wanting What You Want,* and co-author of *The Laws of Lifetime Growth* and *The Advisor Century*.